Alexander S. Pushkin

RUSSIAN TALES

А. Пушкинъ

(1799 – 1837)

ALEXANDER S. PUSHKIN

RUSSIAN TALES

FORUM BOOKS LIMITED

THE
GOLDEN
COCKEREL

In a far and distant land
Many many years ago
Lived a very famous Tsar.
All the borders near his Kingdom
He held secure within his fiefdom.
Fearing nothing, fearing no-one
But growing older he soon tired
Of fighting, and at last desired
Peace and quiet and relaxation
Whereupon to his vexation
All his neighbours promptly rose
And set on him with heavy blows.
To protect the royal borders
From invasion by marauders
He was forced to arm again
Many thousand fighting men.

Though his officers were eager
Their success was only meagre.
They'd go South with fife and drum -
From the East the foe would come!

Then when they had northward turned
In the West the Tsar's land burned!
Tsar Dadon in fury wept
Night and day he never slept.
What a miserable existence!
In despair he sought assistance
From a scholar of great age,
An astrologer and sage.
To him a messenger was sent.

On arrival at the palace
From a sack the scholar old
Took out a cockerel of gold.
"Set this cock upon the steeple,"
Said the scholar, "and he shall
Be your loyal sentinel,
Shall my golden cockerel!
While there's peace along the border
He'll be still, a silent warder.
But the very moment there
Is fuss or danger anywhere,
War, unwelcome visitations,
Hostile strangers, disputations,
Straightaway my Chanticleer
Shall start to crow for all to hear,
Beat his wings to draw attention,
Turn and face the foe's direction."

Tsar Dadon with hope renewed,
And vowing boundless gratitude
To the sage, in exultation
Said: "Such service to the nation
You have rendered that I will
Whatever wish you make fulfil!"

So the cockerel now guarded
All the borders of the Tsardom.
At the slightest sign of strife,
Though fast asleep, he'd spring to life,
Beat his wings to draw attention,
Turn and face the foe's direction,
Crying: "Cock-a-doodle-doodle-doo!
Wake up Tsar Dadon, where are you?"

And so the neighbours, nothing gaining
Grew less keen to go campaigning:
Since they always met rebuff
They very soon had had enough.

For two whole years of peace and plenty
The cock remained a silent sentry.
Then one day a fearful din
Woke Dadon from his sleep within.
"Tsar! My Lord! Our people's father!"
Roared the army's chief commander.
"Woe! Wake up, sire! Woe again!"
"My goodness gracious, gentlemen!"
Said the Tsar and started yawning,
"What's the matter? Who's that calling?"
Came the answer from below:
"Listen to the cockerel crow,
Sowing fear among the people!"
There upon the church's steeple
Stood the cock and never ceased
Loudly crowing, facing East.
Dadon straightaway gave orders:
"On your way there! Mount your horses!"
To the East his elder son
Was sent in haste with fife and drum.
The golden cock then stopped his crowing,
And life again was easy-going.

One by one, eight days elapsed;
From his son came no dispatch,
Not a word in explanation
Of the border situation,
Then the cockerel crowed again.
Tsar Dadon mobilised more men.
His other son leapt on his horse
To lead the second fighting force.

Soon the crowing stopped once more.
But no news came, just as before!
And once again eight days he counted.
Fear among the people mounted.
Then again the cockerel crowed.
This time it was the Tsar who rode
Off to the East. Was it to find
His sons? Would fate be cruel or kind?.

Dadon day and night made haste,
Weary-eyed and solemn faced
But saw no sign of bivouacs
Or campfires; found no battle-axe
Or broken arrow that could say
His two lost sons had passed that way.
The eighth long day was almost spent
When suddenly a silken tent
Appeared to view not far ahead.
Towards it Dadon's carriage sped.
But as he neared the spot his face
Turned pale - it was a fearful place
Fcr men lay slaughtered all around.
And by the silken tent he found
His sons. No sight more grief could bring
To Tsar, or Emperor, or King,
For both lay pale and still, each brother
Pierced by the sword-blade of the other.
Neither wore armour nor bore a shield
And close by on the bloody field
Two patient horses waited for
Their masters who would ride no more.

"O my sons!" Tsar Dadon cried,
"Together fought, together died.
Woe is me! I am undone!
My time to die has also come!"
In the gorge there was a moaning
All the army deeply groaning;
Through the hills a shudder went.
And suddenly by the silken tent
Stood the maiden Queen Shamakha
Fair and lovely, Queen Shamakha
Shining like the morning star,
Softly beckoning to the Tsar.
Like an owl the sunlight reaches,
Hypnotised at once and speechless,
In her presence Tsar Dadon
Clean forgot his two dead sons.

And the Queen serenely smiling
Took his arm and all beguiling
Led him courteously away
Into the tent without delay.
At the table he was seated
Richly fed and sweetly treated;
On a bed of rich brocade
To take his rest the Tsar was laid.
After which, to her dictation
Yielding without reservation,
For a week in rapture rare
Tsar Dadon made merry there.

Seven days Tsar Dadon dallied,
Then at last his men he rallied.
With the maiden at his side
Homeward he began to ride.
Rumour back to town went racing,
Fact and fantasy embracing.
When the Tsar and Queen drew near
Crowds were at the gate to cheer.
People waved, as at a marriage,
Ran along behind the carriage.

Tsar Dadon waved back and bowed.....
Suddenly among the crowd
He saw a figure stooped with age
The wise old man, his friend the sage,
Holding back the crowd at bay.
"Oh, hello there, sir! Good day!"
Called out the Tsar. "And what's your pleasure?
Pray come closer! Speak at leisure!"
"Gracious Tsar!" the sage declared.
"It is time accounts were squared.
For my services, remember,
In resolving your dilemma
You did vow you would fulfil
My wish, whatever I should will
So give me that fair maiden, Lord.
I claim her as my just reward."
At this the Tsar was most surprised.
"Are you serious?!" he cried.
"Clearly, sir, if you continue
In this vein, a devil's in you
Or you're going off your nut!
I, of course, did promise, but
There is a limit! You can't choose her!
And what good is she to you, sir?

That's enough now! Let's talk sense:
What will you have in recompense?
All my gold? A lofty title?
A fine horse with a jewelled bridle?
Half my kingdom? My best slave?"
"It is not for this I crave.
I'll take no other wage or fee -
The maiden there my prize shall be,"
The scholar told him in reply.
Tsar Dadon spat: "No, no, say I!
Nothing - that shall be your portion.
Blame yourself for your misfortune!
Clear off, rascal, while you can!
Be gone from here, you mad old man!"
At this the sage began to wrangle,
Though with some it's rash to tangle;
And the royal mace came down
Upon his forehead. All the town
Shuddered as the old man buckled
And fell dead. The maiden chuckled,
Laughing loudly, full of glee,
Delighting in this villainy.

And the Tsar, although dismayed,
Smiled fawningly upon the maiden.
But as they reached the palace gate
Tsar Dadon felt the air vibrate.
And in full view of all the people
Down the cock flew from the steeple,
Perched upon the Tsar's grey head,
Pecked his pate, then upward fled
Into the sky to disappear
While from the carriage, white with fear,
The Tsar came tumbling down and cried
Out once in agony - then died.
And his fair Queen, like an illusion,
Vanished in the wild confusion.

Not a true tale! But I think
That clever lads can take a hint.

THE
FISHERMAN
AND THE
GOLDEN
FISH

An old man lived with his good-wife
By the shore of the deep blue ocean
In a hovel of clay and wattle:
They had lived there for three years and thirty.
The old man netted fishes,
The good-wife sat at her spinning.

He cast his net once on the water;
The net came up - full of sea-slime.
Again he cast his net;
The net came back - full of sea-weed.
He cast his net for a third time
And it came up with one fish in it,
No common fish, but golden.
The golden fish begged for mercy
And spoke with the voice of a human:
"Old man, throw me back in the ocean,
I will pay you a splendid ransom:
I will grant you whatever you wish for."
The old man was amazed and awestruck:
He had fished here for three years and thirty
And never once heard a fish talking.
Freeing the fish from the meshes
He gave him fair words and gentle:
"Golden fish, go your ways in peace now.
There is no need to pay me a ransom;
Go back to your deep blue waters
And swim there and splash as you please."

The old man returned to his good-wife
And told her of this great wonder:
"Today I netted a strange fish,
No common fish, but golden;
The golden fish spoke our language,
Begged to go home to the ocean,
Promised a splendid ransom:
To grant me whatever I wished for.
I dared not exact the ransom;
Threw him back in the sea for another."
The wife fell to scolding her husband:
"Simpleton, silly old fat-head!
Too soft to take boons from fishes!
A new wash-trough at least you might ask for
Ours is split right down the middle!"

He went back to the deep blue ocean
And saw that the ocean was ruffled.
Then he raised his voice and shouted,
And the golden fish came swimming:
"What is it, old man, come tell me!"
With a low bow, the old man answered:
"Be gracious, Lord of Fishes,
My good-wife is angry with me,
And gives me no peace with her nagging;
She says that we need a new wash-trough;
Ours is split right down the middle."
The golden fish made answer:
"Never mind, old man, go in peace now,
You will find a new wash-trough all ready."

The old man returned to his good-wife
To find the new wash-trough all ready.
But she scolded him worse than ever:
"Simpleton! Silly old fat-head!
So you begged a great boon - a new wash-trough -
But what profit is there in a wash-trough?
Back, you simpleton, go to the great fish,
Make your bow to him: ask for a cottage.

He went back to the deep blue ocean
The ocean was dark now and troubled.
Then he raised his voice and shouted,
And the golden fish came swimming:
"What is it, old man, come, tell me!"
With a low bow, the old man answered:
"Be gracious, Lord of Fishes,
My good-wife is even more angry
And gives me no peace with her nagging:
The old ne'er-content wants a cottage."
The golden fish made answer:
"Never mind, old man, go in peace now,
You shall have your wish: a new cottage."

The old man returned to his hovel...
Not a trace remained of the hovel:
In its place - a brand-new cottage
With a whitewashed, brickwork chimney,
Oaken doors and shuttered windows.
On the garden seat sat his good-wife
Quite beside herself this time with anger:
"What a fool you are, simpleton, fat-head!
So you begged a great boon, a low cottage!
Go back, make your bow to the great fish:
I will not be a plain peasant woman,
Let him make me a high-born lady."

The old man went down to the ocean
The ocean was rough now and choppy.
Then he raised his voice and shouted,
And the golden fish came swimming:
"What is it, old man, come, tell me!"
With a low bow, the old man answered:
"Be gracious, Lord of Fishes!
My good-wife's more angry than ever
And gives me no peace with her nagging;
And now she has taken a notion
That she'll not be a plain peasant woman
But will be a high-born lady."
The golden fish made answer:
"Never mind, old man, go in peace now."

The old man returned to his good-wife.
And what did he see? A fine mansion.
In the porch his good-wife standing,
In a rich jacket trimmed with sable,
A high, brocaded head-dress,
Pearls on her neck hanging heavy,
Gold rings upon her fingers
And boots of soft, red leather.
Before her, servants bowing;
While she pulled their hair and stroke them.
The old man hailed his good-wife:
"How now, Mistress-Madam-M'lady,
Surely your heart is content now?"
His good-wife greeted him harshly,
And sent him to work in the stables.

A week went by, then another,
And the good-wife, more self-willed than ever,
Sent the old man back to the ocean.
"Go back, make your bow to the great fish:
Say I'll not be a high-born lady.
Let him make me a mighty Empress."
The old man took fright, and argued:
"What, woman! You must be moon-struck!
You talk and you walk like a fishwife:
You will set your whole Empire laughing."
The good-wife grew still more angry,
Boxed her husband's ears and shouted:
"How dare you argue, you peasant,
With me, with a high-born lady?
Get you gone to the sea, I tell you,
Unless you want to be dragged there."

The old man went back to the ocean
Black and threatening now, the blue ocean.
Then he raised his voice and shouted,
And the golden fish came swimming:
"What is it, old man, come, tell me!"
With a low bow, the old man answered:
"Be gracious, Lord of Fishes!
Again my good-wife's on the rampage;
This time she's taken a notion
That she'll not be a high-born lady
But will be a mighty Empress."
And the golden fish made answer:
"Never mind, old man, go in peace now!
You will find your good-wife an Empress!"

The old man returned to his good-wife.
And what do you think? A palace
Now housed the shrewish old woman.
She sat in state at her table.
Great nobles and lords waiting on her,
Serving her wine in a golden goblet
While she nibbled at cakes and sweetmeats;
Stern sentries on guard about her,
Each with an axe at the ready.
The old man took one look - his poor knees buckled.
He bowed before her
But he spoke out: "Hail, dread Empress!
Tell me, is your heart content now?"
Not a glance did his good-wife spare him
But ordered her men to remove him.
Then the lords and great nobles came running.
By the scruff of his neck they took him
And the sentries who stood in the doorways
Saw him off with their glinting axes,
And the people mocked him with laughter:
"Serve you right, old witless grey-beard!
Let that be a lesson to you
To remember your place in future!"

So a week went by, then another.
The old woman grew more and more grasping.
She sent courtiers to fetch the old man.
They found him and brought him before her.
Then the good-wife said to her husband:
"Go back, make your bow to the great fish.
I'll no more be a mighty Empress
But will rule over Sea and Ocean.
In the Deep I will make my stronghold
And the golden fish shall serve me
And swim back and forth on my errands."

The old man dared not contradict her,
Was afraid to stand up against her.
So again he went down to the ocean
And saw - a black storm had arisen:
Angry waves reared up to meet him,
All a-quake, all a-swirl, all a-roaring.
But he raised his voice and shouted,
And the golden fish came swimming:
"What is it, old man, come, tell me!"
With a low bow, the old man answered:
"Be gracious, Lord of Fishes!
What can I do with the woman?
The old fool will no longer be Empress,
But will rule over Sea and Ocean;
In the Deep she will make her stronghold
And have you yourself to serve her
And swim back and forth on her errands."
The golden fish said nothing;
With a flick of its tail in the water
It swam away, back to the deep sea.

The old man by the shore stood waiting
For a long time, but got no answer.
At last, he returned to his good-wife
And lo! There she sat on the threshold
Of their old hut of clay and wattle
And before her - the broken wash-trough.

THE PRIEST AND HIS WORKMAN BALDA

Once there was a stupid priest
A simpleton, to say the least,

Who to the market went one day
And strolled around in some dismay.

Here a wise old peasant found him
Balda was what the town's folk called him.

"Good-day, your Honour," said the man
"I'd like to help you if I can."
Said he: "A servant I require
A cook, a groom, a carpenter,
But nowadays it's hard to find such
A man who doesn't cost too much."
"Good Sire," said Balda, "I'll work for you
Loyally, diligently, cheaply too.
For wages, just my daily meal
And one more thing to clinch the deal:

Three flicks with my fingers on your brow
Once a year. Shall we shake on it now?"
The priest wondered: "Can there be a catch?"
And gave his big dumb head a scratch.
But he wanted a servant, a cheap one too,
And reckoned that Balda ought to do.
So he shook Balda's hand and said: "By God,
I agree to the bargain, so come with me.
You say you work hard: well now, let's see."

So Balda moved in. His bed was of straw.
He rose each day when the clock struck four.
After his meal, while the house was still drowsing,
He'd harness the horses and do the ploughing,
Light the stove long before anyone asked him,
Do the chores, boil the eggs, and even shell them.
The priest's wife thought he was wonderful,
And Balda was fond of their little girl;
The priest's little boy called Balda "daddy",
And Balda was nice to the spoilt little laddie.
Only the priest disliked the poor man
Always finding fault, as some people can.
As time passed he thought with mounting fear
Of the fast-approaching end of the year.
Appetite, thirst and sleep all left him -
Already his forehead began to hurt him.
"Can you see a way out?", he begged his wife.
"When I think of that brute I fear for my life."
Now she was a woman of nasty guile
Accustomed to every kind of wile.
She told him, "I think I know of a way
To keep this disaster firmly at bay:
Set Balda a task that he cannot do,
But insist that he fulfil it for you.
Your forehead to no harm will come
And Balda can just go suck his thumb."
Much comforted by this idea
The priest faced Balda without any fear
And shouted: "Balda, quick as you can,
Come here, you miserable man.
Those Sea-Devils they are bound to give
Me quit-rent for as long as I live:
This has always been our little arrangement,
But for three years now there's been no payment.
So finish your porridge, then off you go
And bring me back the money they owe."
It was useless to argue, thought Balda, so he
Dashed off straightaway and stood by the sea.

He whipped at the water with a long rope
Till it foamed and bubbled just like soap.
Of course, a Sea-Devil rose up to complain:
"What ever's the matter? Kindly explain,"
He said. Said Balda, "I'm flogging the sea
So that you'll come up and listen to me."
The old Sea Devil was quite downcast.
"What have you got against us?" he asked.

What indeed? Why, you're not paying the rent
You owe. It is really quite negligent.
So I'll have some fun, on that you can bet,
And you Sea-Devils will just have to sweat."
"Please, dear Balda, don't flog the sea
You'll soon be paid, just trust in me.
My grandson will come and talk to you."
"And try," thought Balda, "to fool me too!"
The imp came up as he was bidden,
Prancing about like a new-born kitten.

He called out: "Balda, Sir, hello!
What quit-rent is it you say we owe?
We've heard nothing of it for ages
So why on earth have you come back to plague us?
But since you insist there's a debt we owe
We should settle this matter, and then you can go.
And so to these terms let us now agree:
Whoever runs fastest around the sea
Can go and pick up the full amount
That my brothers just are now beginning to count."
On hearing this Balda gave a big laugh:
"Can any-one really be so daft?
Do you really think, little imp, that I -
Big bold Balda - with you should vie?
Is it wise to pit your strength against me?
It's a stupid challenge, you wait and see!"
And off he went to the wood and caught
Two lively young hares, and these he brought
In a sack to the edge of the shore. And then
He said to the imp, "Just listen again."
He held up one of the hares by the ears.
"You haven't a chance against one of my years

And I see little imp, that you're too weak
To seriously think you can compete
With me. Anyhow I've no time to waste
And first with my brother you'll have to race.
On your marks, get set, and off you go!"
Away dashed the imp and Balda's hare, so
The little imp ran as fast as he could
While the hare raced back to its home in the wood.
Fast round the sea the little imp sped,
Puffing and panting, his face a deep red.
When he got back he was covered in sweat -
His tailfeathers even were soaking wet.
But he thought: "Now Balda is really done for."
Yet there sat Balda, stroking his brother
The hare, saying gently, "Here my dearie,
Rest for a while. You must be weary."
So the imp thought the hare must have really won
Even though he was sure he'd not seen him run.
"I'll go for the rent," he said in a hush,
And back to his grandad he went in a rush.
"Balda's brother ran faster than I," he said
The Sea-Devil's face looked as heavy as lead

So angry was he. He fell into deep thought
While above him old Balda such havoc wrought,
That the sea was set surging and splashing:
Wild waves rose up, then fell roaring and crashing.
The imp came back: "Please stop and you will be sent
All the money that's due for your master's quit-rent.
But listen a moment. Do you see this stick?
Well, wherever you fancy, - come just take your pick -
And whoever can throw it the hardest and furthest
Can claim the quit-rent - I mean this in earnest.
Or is it too heavy?" Said Balda, "Oh, no:
I am just waiting for my turn to throw
It over that cloud. And then I shall start
On you, little imp, so you'd better look smart!"
Then imp scuttled back to his home to complain
That old man Balda had won - yet again.

And once again Balda took up his long lash
And threatened to give the Sea-Devils a thrash.
Begged the imp: "Oh no, please, you are scaring us stiff.
I'll get you the quit-rent at once, Balda, if..."
"I'll have no more of that nonsense, Imp," Balda said.
"You must listen to me just for once now instead.
Now it's my turn the rules of the contest to choose
And once more, you horrible villain, you'll lose.
Do you see that mare yonder? Well if you can lift
Her I'll give you the rent that you owe as a gift,
But if you can't do it, the rent's mine, of course.
So come, little imp - can you lift up that horse?"
The poor little devil then heaved a great sigh
And crawled under the mare. He gave it a try,
And puffing and panting with hustle and bustle,
Straining away at each sinew and muscle,
He picked up the mare - but alas and alack!
Collapsed in a heap with the mare on his back.

"Oh, what a silly young imp you must be
Even to think that you could outsmart me,"
Said Balda. "Now look, and you'll see with what ease
I can carry the mare..... right between my knees."
And he jumped on the mare (as a good rider may
When he knows how to ride) and he galloped away.

Home the imp ran once again to complain
That old man Balda had won yet again.
The Devils gave in, put the rent in a sack
And grudgingly placed it upon Balda's back.

Off he went, grunting and bent over double.
The priest saw him coming and quickly sensed trouble.
Trembling and fearful once more for his life
He tried hard to shelter behind his wife,
But Balda espied him. "This is for you,"
He said, and then he demanded his due.

The poor priest offered
His stupid brow:
At the first flick
He flew to the ceiling;
The next
Left him speechless, reeling;
The third flick stripped
Him of his wits,
While Balda said, "That's what you reap
For trying to get your work done dirt cheap."

The End

CONTENTS

First published in 1990 by Forum Books Limited
Little Heath Road, Chobham, Surrey GU24 8RL
England

Original Russian language edition published by
Malysh Publishers, Moscow.

English Translation:
The Golden Cockerel by Peter Tempest.
The Fisherman and the Golden Fish by Avril Pyman.
The Priest and his Workman Balda by Louis Zellikov.

Printed in the Soviet Union

ISBN 1-872081-06-1